S0-CCD-953

WINTER IN CANADA

Machines

Nicole Mortillaro

Scholastic Canada Ltd.
Toronto New York London Auckland Sydney
Mexico City New Delhi Hong Kong Buenos Aires

Scholastic Canada Ltd.
604 King Street West, Toronto, Ontario M5V 1E1, Canada

Scholastic Inc.
557 Broadway, New York, NY 10012, USA

Scholastic Australia Pty Limited
PO Box 579, Gosford, NSW 2250, Australia

Scholastic New Zealand Limited
Private Bag 94407, Botany, Manukau 2163, New Zealand

Scholastic Children's Books
Euston House, 24 Eversholt Street, London NW1 1DB, UK

www.scholastic.ca

Library and Archives Canada Cataloguing in Publication

Mortillaro, Nicole, 1972-, author
Machines / Nicole Mortillaro.
(Winter in Canada)
ISBN 978-1-4431-5765-0 (softcover)
1. Snow removal--Equipment and supplies--Juvenile literature.
2. Ice prevention and control--Equipment and supplies--Juvenile
literature. 3. Snowmaking--Equipment and supplies--Juvenile
literature. 4. Snowmobiles--Juvenile literature. 5. Zambonis
(Trademark)--Juvenile literature. I. Title.
TD868.M67 2017   j625.7'63   C2017-901516-8

Developed and Produced by Focus Strategic Communications Inc.
Project Management and Editorial: Adrianna Edwards, Ron Edwards
Design and Layout: Ruth Dwight
Photo Research: Adrianna Edwards, Ron Edwards, Paula Joiner
Copyediting and Proofreading: Francine Geraci
Fact Checking: Wendy Scavuzzo

Visual Credits

Photos ©: cover: KKIDD/iStockphoto; back cover: Ken Gillespie/Design Pics Inc./Alamy Images; back cover snow, 1-2: TungCheung/Shutterstock; 4: huseyintuncer/iStockphoto; 5 top: P. Dionne/Peche et Océans Canada; 5 bottom: VisualCommunications/iStockphoto; 6: Photo courtesy of Canadian Pacific; 7 top: Pep Roig/Alamy Images; 7 bottom: Lebracht Music and Arts Photo Library/Alamy Images; 8: Dragos Iliescu/Shutterstock; 9 top: CHROMORANGE/Hans Eder/Alamy Images; 9 bottom: Elena Elisseeva/Alamy Images; 10: USGS/U.S. Geological Survey; 11 top: Ken Gillespie/Design Pics Inc./Alamy Images; 11 bottom left: Hannes Rada/Getty Images; 11 bottom right: blickwinkel/Rose/Alamy Images; 12-13 bottom: Courtesy of the Greater Toronto Airports Authority; 13 top: Daniel Jedzura/Shutterstock; 14: Courtesy of the Greater Toronto Airports Authority; 15 top: shaunl/iStockphoto; 15 bottom: Philippe Henry/Design Pics Inc./Alamy Images; 16: nikitos77/iStockphoto; 17 top: ZUMA Press, Inc./ Alamy Images; 17 bottom left: Aigars Reinholds/Shutterstock; 17 bottom right: LUNNA TOWNSHIP/ Shutterstock; 18: Ivan Smuk/Alamy Images; 19 top: Dmitry Naumov/Shutterstock; 19 bottom: Shotshop GmbH/Alamy Images; 20: Petr Bonek/Alamy Images; 21 top: Marco Barone/Shutterstock; 21 bottom: Petr Bonek/Alamy Images; 22: Steve CollenderShutterstock; 23 top: MTA/Alamy Images; 23 bottom: Robert Hoetink/Shutterstock; 24: Wolfgang Kaehler/Superstock, Inc.; 25 top: David Gowans/Alamy Images; 25 bottom: Kurt and Rosalia Scholz/Superstock, Inc.; 26: Nate Allred/ Shutterstock; 27 top: Jacques Boissinot/Canadian Press Images; 27 centre: FPW/Alamy Images; 27 bottom: Nino Marcutti/Alamy Images; 28: GerryRousseau/Alamy Images; 29 top: Canonman29/ Dreamstime; 29 bottom: andybrannan/iStockphoto; 30: katatonia82/Shutterstock; 31 top: Vadym Sarakhan/Dreamstime; 31 bottom: bbbb/Shutterstock.

Copyright © 2017 by Scholastic Canada Ltd.
All rights reserved.

No part of this publication may be reproduced or stored in a retrieval system, or transmitted in any form or by any means, electronic, mechanical, recording, or otherwise, without written permission of the publisher, Scholastic Canada Ltd., 604 King Street West, Toronto, Ontario M5V 1E1, Canada. In the case of photocopying or other reprographic copying, a licence must be obtained from Access Copyright (Canadian Copyright Licensing Agency), 56 Wellesley Street West, Suite 320, Toronto, Ontario M5S 2S3 (1-800-893-5777).

6 5 4 3 2 1   Printed in Malaysia 108   17 18 19 20 21 22

TABLE OF CONTENTS

LET IT SNOW!

Canada is one of the snowiest countries in the world, and one of the coldest. Many communities across the country get more than 100 cm of snow a year. But if you live in Iqaluit, Nunavut, you get almost 230 cm a year!

All that snow can make it hard for people and goods to get around. Good thing we have tough machines to help us! Buckle up and meet these cool machines — ones that can smash through ice, push piles of snow or blast it away. Other special vehicles — those that polish rinks, groom snow or zoom over it at high speeds — help us have tons of winter fun.

COLD, HARD FACTS

- The lowest temperature ever recorded in North America was at the village of Snag, Yukon: –63°C on February 3, 1947.

- Canada's biggest snowfall in a 24-hour period — 145 cm — happened in Tahtsa Lake, British Columbia, in 1999.

- After a 1998 storm dumped up to 100 mm of ice pellets and freezing rain on much of the St. Lawrence Valley, the Canadian Forces sent more than 15 000 troops to the area to restore power and provide emergency shelter and medical aid.

TRAIN PLOWS

In order for trains to run in winter, they need a clear path free of snow. These huge plows remove snow from railway tracks by pushing it or blowing it away.

A **wedge** plow has a horizontal wedge that lifts the snow upward while a vertical wedge pushes the snow to the side. It takes a lot of force to move snow in this way, and sometimes it's difficult to manage in deep drifts.

That's where a **rotary** snowplow comes in. It has 10 blades that throw snow 30 m away. And those blades spin pretty fast! They can turn 60 to 90 times per minute.

The smooth surface of the wedge plow allows snow to slide off the plow's face rather than sticking to it.

blades

The rotary snowplow can carve its way through mountains of snow.

◄ Rotary snowplows have been keeping railway tracks clear since the 19th century.

MADE IN CANADA

- The first rotary snowplow was designed by a Toronto dentist named J. W. Elliot. His design was improved by another Canadian, Orange Jull, a few years later.

- The **prototype** was built by brothers Edward and John Leslie, of Orangeville, Ontario, in the early 1880s. It was tested and approved by the Canadian Pacific Railway in 1883–1884.

SNOW BLOWERS

Many Canadians live with snow for as much as half of the year. And in that time the snow can really pile up.

We need to put that snow somewhere. We have developed many ways of moving snow so that we can get around more easily. Blowing snow is the easiest way to get rid of it. The blades of a snow blower push the snow into a **chute** that blows the snow away. Snow blowers are everywhere in Canada, clearing streets, sidewalks and even our driveways!

chute →

blades

◄ Smaller snow blowers clear paths
where the big machines can't go!

MADE IN CANADA

In 1925, Arthur Sicard of Sainte-Thérèse,
Quebec (a small town northwest of
Montreal) invented the first practical
snow blower. Sicard's snow blower was
mounted on a truck with a separate
motor to shoot the snow through a chute.
It could throw snow over 25 m away!

ICEBREAKERS

Because Canada is a northern country, much of its water freezes over for many months of the year. Icebreakers clear paths through sea and river ice. To do that, icebreaker ships have to have extra-strong **hulls** that are **reinforced** and weighted so they can smash through thick ice. Most have specially designed hulls shaped to push the broken ice down, out of their path. They ram into the ice, and are forced up on top of it. The weight of the reinforced hull crashes down and through the hard, thick ice. These ships also need very powerful engines to be able to do this. Without these features, icebreakers could easily be trapped in the ice, which would be a huge danger to both ship and crew. If one were to become stuck, the tremendous **pressure** of the ice could crush the ship.

The CCGS *Louis S. St-Laurent* is Canada's biggest icebreaker, and in 1993 it was the first Canadian ship to reach the North Pole.

Amphibious excavators (such as this one shown on the Red River in Manitoba) break up ice. This helps to prevent spring flooding.

In both the Arctic and Antarctic, icebreakers are used to deliver equipment and supplies. ▼

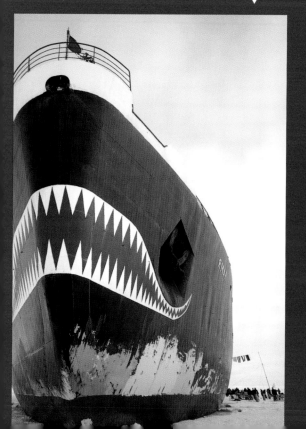

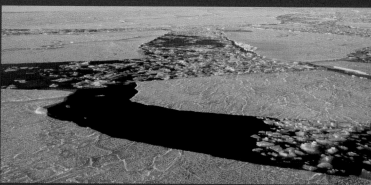

▲ Icebreakers clear paths through the ice for shipping vessels.

COAST GUARD CONFIDENTIAL

- The Canadian Coast Guard Service (CCGS) has 17 icebreakers, ranging in size from 28 m to 120 m long.

- Some CCGS icebreakers do double duty as scientific research ships in summer.

DE-ICERS

Imagine being in a tiny cab, high above a huge jet plane. That's what people who work de-icing machines do. These machines blast a mixture of chemicals onto an airplane to melt any ice that has frozen onto it. De-icing must be done right before takeoff so that the plane does not ice up again. Ice and snow buildup adds extra weight. It also interferes with airflow over the wings and the plane's ability to lift off properly.

De-icing trucks have a hydraulic lift that carries the operator high above the plane. The trucks also have pumps that carry the de-icing fluid through the hoses to the top of the lift, where the operator then sprays the plane with it. The plane quickly taxis to the runway for takeoff. If the plane has to wait too long, the de-icing must be done over again!

operator

cab

hydraulic lift

hose

truck

De-icing a plane can take anywhere from two to twenty minutes.

De-icing fluid is often a bright colour so that operators can see where it is being sprayed. It is also very slippery! A de-icer carries about 7500 L of fluid.

SNOWPLOWS

Snowplows help us to push snow off roads so that we can travel safely from place to place. Dump trucks and other summer construction machines don't get a break. In the winter, they are fitted with plows on the front and get to work on the snow.

There are several styles of plows. V-plows are best at breaking through hard packed snow, ice and deep snow drifts. Straight plows have a flat blade, mounted at an angle, and are good at clearing a wide path of snow by pushing it off to the side. Box plows, also known as containment plows, collect snow inside the scoop and don't create snowbanks along the sides of the plow.

Large highways are often cleared of snow by several plows driving side by side in **ranks**. There are huge, specialized machines to clear large surfaces such as airport runways. Small, compact tractors clear sidewalks and other narrow spaces.

Airport snowplows are the widest and move at a maximum speed of 40 km/h.

Huge plows are mounted on heavy trucks (like this dump truck) to remove snow from roads.

blade

Small snowplows like this one can clear snow from sidewalks and other areas where larger equipment cannot go. ▼

PUSHY PLOWS

- The first snowplows were made of wood and pulled by horses.

- Some provinces use articulated snowplows, which can clear two lanes of a highway at once!

- Snowplow blades come in different sizes. They range from 1.2 m blades for ATVs and other small vehicles to the full-sized 8.4 m blades.

SNOW-REMOVAL MACHINES

Canada gets a lot of snow most winters, and it can really pile up. We plow it, we blow it, we shovel it and we pour salt and other chemicals on it to melt it away. Snowplows move tons of snow off our busy streets, sidewalks and highways. There it piles up in snowbanks. After a while, those mounds of snow get bigger and bigger, higher and higher. During cold winters, very little of that snow melts, and it builds up along the sides of roads and walkways.

That can be a serious problem, especially in cities where road and sidewalk space is limited to begin with. Many Canadian cities get rid of the snow by hauling it away. Snow blowers and backhoes load the snow into trucks that take it away to dump sites, keeping streets and walkways clear.

Backhoes pick up and shovel snow into dump trucks that haul it away to dump sites.

Snow removed from city streets gets put in a snow dump site. Sometimes these mountains of snow don't melt away until summer.

A Bobcat excavator removes snow from city sidewalks and other places a big machine cannot fit.

An average dump truck can haul away 60 bathtubs worth of snow at a time. ▶

SNOW-MAKING EQUIPMENT

Canada is one of the coldest and snowiest countries in the world. But that doesn't mean we get snow all the time. Ski resorts need a deep base of snow so that people can ski and snowboard, even when it gets warmer. So what do you do when you need more snow? You make it, of course!

Snow guns are placed along the sides of a ski hill and connected to water pipes or hoses, usually buried underground. Water is pumped into the snow gun and forced out through tiny holes, making a fine spray. A fan — or sometimes **compressed** air — blows the spray up into the air and out onto the hill. The fine spray freezes by the time it hits the ground, creating a fresh blanket of snow, ready for when we hit the slopes.

This snow cannon uses a fan and can make a greater amount of snow faster than a snow lance.

A snow lance has a long, thin metal tube and uses compressed air to blast the spray out.

FAKE SNOW FACTS

- Snow-making works best when it is –12°C with low **humidity**. The colder and drier it is, the better the snow.

- In its highest snow-making year, British Columbia's Whistler Blackcomb ski area made more than one billion litres of snow.

- Machine-made snow looks like little round balls, not like natural six-sided snowflake crystals.

SNOW GROOMERS

With all the snow that falls in Canada, it's no wonder we love to ski. But it takes more than just snow to make a great ski hill. Sometimes ski hills can get bumpy or uneven. That's when snow **groomers** come in. These machines smooth out rough patches so that the hills are safer for skiers. They can also create snowboarding areas.

Snow groomers use a **continuous** track system like a tank, but the tracks of a snow groomer are made of rubber. A shovel or blade at the front shaves down bumps and moves snow to where it needs to be. A roller at the back smooths the snow and evens out the texture.

Different types of snow groomers do different things. Some groom for cross-country skiing, some for snowmobiling and others for snowshoeing.

If you've never seen a snow groomer, there's a reason: they usually work at night when there are no skiers around!

The weight of the snow groomer is spread across the treads, preventing it from sinking into the snow.

cab

roller

shovel or blade

wheels and treads

LOOKING SNOW GOOD!

- Groomers can build up mounds of snow, but downhill skiers can also form **moguls** when they make their turns.

- There are over 500 cross-country ski areas across Canada, and many of these are groomed by machine.

- Groomers smooth out cross-country or snowmobile trails, leaving corduroy-shaped ridges.

SNOW MELTERS

We've seen different methods to get snow out of the road, including snow blowers and snowplows. But there is yet another way to get rid of snow. We can melt it!

Snow melters use hot water or flame burners to get rid of a pile of snow. **Stationary** melters stay put — the snow has to be brought to them (usually in trucks) for melting. **Mobile** melters are mounted on wheels with an engine that allows them to go to the snow and melt it. These machines are used to keep roads, airport runways and other surfaces clear of snow.

Salt trucks use road salt to melt ice and snow. Salt is stored in a **hopper** at the back of the truck, and a **rotor** spreads the salt over roads, parking lots and sidewalks.

Snow is scooped up and dumped into a stationary snow-melting machine.

A mobile snow melter uses heat to blast away snow on a railway track.

Every winter, machines like this spread salt over roads and sidewalks to melt snow and ice.

MELTING AWAY FACTS

- Snow melters often have **filters** or screens to catch solids so they don't pollute storm drains.

- Snow melters save the cost of trucking and storing the snow until it melts in warmer weather.

- One of the most common ice melters is not a machine — it's salt. Salt lowers the freezing temperature of ice and snow, so it melts at temperatures below 0°C.

SKI PLANES

Most planes take off and land on a runway. But the ones that fly people and supplies to remote locations in the winter need to be able to land on snow. Instead of having wheels to land on, these planes are fitted with skis — just like you might wear when you go skiing yourself. The propeller or jet engine pushes these planes forward during takeoff. For landing, they just glide along on their skis.

The skis used on these planes are special. They can be moved up and down. They are coated with a slippery finish that stops snow from sticking to them when they are parked. All sorts of planes use skis when flying in snowy weather. These include the tiny Piper Cub, the giant Lockheed C-130 and the Canadian-built Twin Otter.

The wide skis help spread the plane's weight so it doesn't sink down in the snow.

The giant Lockheed C-130's wingspan is 40 m. That's almost as long as an Olympic-sized swimming pool! They have flown in the Arctic and Antarctic.

MADE IN CANADA

Canada's legendary, dependable de Havilland Twin Otter is used around the world. Of the 844 original planes built between 1965 and 1988, more than half are still flying today.

In 2016, two Canadian Twin Otter ski planes, similar to the one pictured here, were used to rescue sick scientists stuck at a research outpost in Antarctica. ▲

SNOWMOBILES

Snowmobiles make it possible for people to get around in areas with heavy snow and limited roadways. Snowmobiles are also great for fun and games. Lots of people enjoy snowmobile trail riding and racing, which is an important part of the tourism **industry** for many northern communities.

Snowmobiles have handlebars that you steer like a bicycle. The engine drives the **crank**, which rotates the wheels that are connected to the treads. The treads bite into the snow and push the snowmobile forward on the two skis in the front.

Snowmobiles can be a lifeline in some areas, where police, health workers, mail carriers and regular people rely on them to get around when roads are not **passable** after heavy snowfalls or ice storms.

Snowmobiles are also used for fun. There are about 137 000 km of marked and maintained trails across Canada.

Police officers often rely on snowmobiles to patrol, respond to calls and get around in winter months.

◄ Bombardier's B7 model snowmobile was first built in 1939, had treads like those on tanks, an enclosed cabin for passengers and a car engine. It could carry seven passengers, which is how it got its name.

BOMBARDIER

Joseph-Armand Bombardier lived in Valcourt, Quebec, which is east of Montreal. Winters in Valcourt were harsh, and snow often clogged the roads. In 1934, Bombardier's son Yvon became sick and died because no one was able to get through the snow to take him to hospital. This tragedy motivated Bombardier to invent the snowmobile.

ICE RESURFACERS

Skating and hockey are popular pastimes in Canada. And the ice surfaces we use require specialized care so that we can enjoy them. As we skate, our blades cut into the ice, making it bumpy. In the past it took a team of workers to scrape away all the ice chips and debris and smooth out the ice. That took a lot of time and skill.

Then along came Frank Zamboni. He operated an ice-skating rink in southern California and knew a lot about ice and refrigeration. In 1949, he invented a machine to fix the ice-surfacing problem. It shaves the ice, then sprays water that freezes into a smooth surface. Today the ice resurfacer is used in just about every hockey and skating arena worldwide.

An ice resurfacer cleans an indoor ice rink during the 2010 Winter Olympics in Vancouver.

It usually takes six to seven minutes to resurface a typical hockey rink.

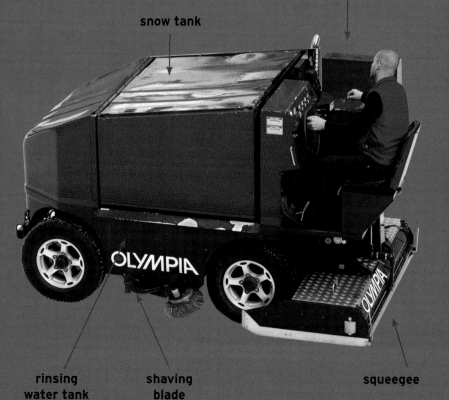

snow tank

washing
water tank

rinsing
water tank

shaving
blade

squeegee

OLYMPIA

HOW IT WORKS

- An ice resurfacer shaves a thin layer off the surface of the ice with a shaving blade.

- Ice shavings are scooped up, and screw-shaped blades push them into the snow tank.

- Tanks hold the water used to wash and rinse the ice.

- Water is spread across the ice. A squeegee spreads it evenly.

ALL-TERRAIN VEHICLES (ATVS)

In a country with a lot of snow and several months of winter, many Canadians don't like being cooped up at home for such a long time. So we've found unique ways of having fun. Forget skating or skiing: we're using machines!

An all-terrain vehicle, or ATV, is a machine that can travel through all kinds of off-road conditions or terrain. These machines can travel through rocky areas, wet areas and, yes, even snow.

Winter ATVs need to be equipped with special tires or tracks, which allow them to get a good grip in ice and snow. Now it's time to have some fun!

Some ATVs use special tires for winter, while others have tank-like tracks that let them travel over snow.

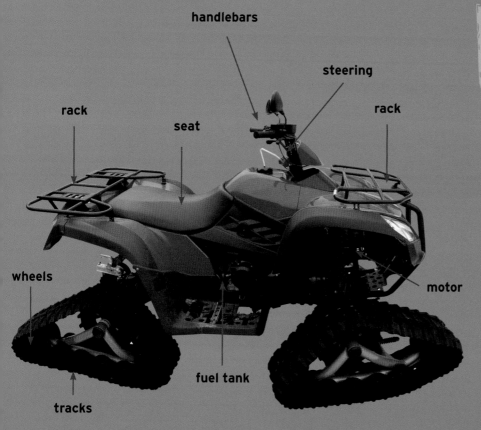

handlebars

steering

rack

rack

seat

wheels

motor

fuel tank

tracks

GET A GRIP

- Vehicles that drive through snow should use special snow tires. These tires stay soft in the cold so that they can grip the road.

- ATV tires have really thick treads, so they get a better grip on the slippery snow.

- Some ATVs have tracks like those on a tank. They provide even better grip on snow.

GLOSSARY

amphibious: Able to travel on land and in water

cab: The driver's area of a large truck or machine

chute: A narrow, tilted passage for sending things like garbage, laundry, grain, or snow to another level

compressed: Something that is pressed or flattened together in order to fit into a smaller space

continuous: Present or happening all the time without stopping

crank: A handle that is attached at a right angle to a shaft and is turned to make a machine work

filter: A device that cleans liquids or gases as they pass through it

fluid: A substance that can flow, such as a liquid or gas

groomer: A machine or person that maintains the cleanliness or appearance of something

hopper: A funnel-shaped container for delivering and storing material, such as grain

hull: The frame or body of a ship, boat or aircraft

humidity: The amount of moisture in the air

hydraulic: machinery that is operated by the pressure that results when a liquid (such as water) is forced through a tube

industry: The businesses that provide a particular product or service

mobile: Able to move or be moved easily

mogul: A small, hard mound of snow on a ski slope

passable: Clear of obstacles and able to be traveled on

pressure: The force produced by pressing on something, as in water pressure

prototype: The first version of an invention that tests an idea to see if it will work

rank: A lineup, arranged in an orderly row

reinforce: Make stronger

rotar: The part of an engine or other machine that turns

rotary: Turning on a central point like a wheel; having a rotating part

stationary: Non-moving

taxi: To go at low speed (as a plane) along the surface of the ground or water

wedge: A piece of food, wood, plastic or metal that is thin and pointed at one end and thick at the other